SUMMARY

Educated

A Memoir

Tara Westover

Learnify.me

Before we proceed…

Feel free to follow us on social media to be notified of future summaries.

1- *Facebook: BookSummaries*
   https://www.facebook.com/BookSummaries-1060732983986564/

2- *Instagram: BookSummaries*
   https://www.instagram.com/booksummaries/

Do you enjoy discussing your thoughts on books you read or what others are reading? Join our Facebook group for discussion, book recommendation, and occasional freebies.

https://www.facebook.com/groups/740824996041852/

TABLE OF CONTENTS

INTRODUCTION

Thank you for purchasing _Educated: A Memoir_ book summary! This summary contains shorter version of the original book. If you want to read full content and if you are satisfied with the summary, go and purchase the original book!

Education: A Memoir is an autobiographical book written by young female author, Tara Westover. Although some readers may wonder at the authenticity of the book since the author is a bit "too young to write an autobiography," the quality of written content is without question.

As the reader reads, they will have the opportunity to get to know Tara, her personal life, her past and her present. Growing up in a Mormon family, her life was without electricity, in addition to poor education and medical care, Tara's life was filled with many difficulties even before she started living it. However, regardless of that, Tara showed to the world that it is possible to succeed, regardless of how poor, unfortunate and difficult the situation in which one lives, is. Forty chapters, which are easy and quick to read, but interesting and compelling, _"Educated: A Memoir"_ is the type of book that is destined to leave a mark in the lives of every reader.

SUMMARY

PART 1: ALWAYS CHOOSING THE GOOD

In the first chapter of the book, we are introduced to Tara's father Gene, and her maternal grandmother. The author describes Gene's commanding attitude, his working life, and his zealous and narrow-minded religious view of the world. Here we also read that Gene's opinion regarding his children often came into conflict with the opinion of their grandmother. She wanted her grandchildren to attend school rather to roam the mountain like savages.

As we read the chapter, we see more descriptions of Tara's father, his narrow views on the world in general and in particular. We read how Gene used to scare the children by telling them horrible and untrue stories about the American government and the Feds. At the end of the chapter, we can read more about their life in the wild. We read how children were instructed to behave if (and when) the Feds attacked them.

PART 2: BEING A MIDWIFE

In the second chapter, the author writes about the practice of something called "midwifery." We read that this practice existed in rural parts of Idaho and that Tara's mother Faye had become a midwife.

Being a midwife was not illegal. However, every midwife risked charges for practicing medicine without a license if a delivery went wrong and mother or child died. Because of that, not many women wanted to become midwives. Tara's mother was a skilled herbalist and midwife's assistant and after some time, she was the only midwife in the region.

Gene supported the idea of midwives because he strongly believed that hospitals were actually agents of corruption and that they were used for brainwashing. Faye used some of the money she made for buying an oxygen tank and for a suturing class. Here we read that the author often accompanied her mother to deliveries but that she did not enjoy the experience.

Later in this chapter, we also read how Faye started to oppose Gene's wishes.

PART 3: MOTHER LARUE

In chapter three, readers find out some more about Faye and her mother, LaRue, Tara's grandmother. We also read that LaRue's father had been an alcoholic. As a result, Tara's grandmother suffered from social contempt. When LaRue got married, she wanted to make sure that her daughter (Faye) would avoid the same fate. Since LaRue was one of the best tailors in the valley, she made beautiful clothes for Faye. LaRue wanted to make sure that her family would be as socially respectable as possible.

We also read how Faye fell in love with Gene. Gene was a man whose life and personality were shaped by life in mountains. The author wrote here how her mother was captivated to the point of obsession by the sovereignty and privacy she could find by living in the mountains.

Later in this chapter, we read some more about Gene and his ways of living.

PART 4: PLANS TO ESCAPE TO ARIZONA

Here in this chapter, the author reminisces on her family plan to go to Arizona in order to avoid the cold winter. However, their trip to Arizona was prevented by a road accident. Tara's then-seventeen-year-old brother fell asleep while driving. While Tara and her younger siblings were not seriously hurt, Faye suffered a brain injury and Tyler, her brother who was driving, smashed his front teeth. Gene considered taking Faye to the hospital, but later changed his mind.

Faye did recover, but Tyler was consumed with guilt. Every time his mother would display memory loss, he would remember the accident.

PART 5: TYLER LEAVING HOME

In chapter five, we read how Tyler, Tara's older brother left their home. Instead of choosing manual labor like his older brothers, Tony and Shawn, Tyler instead wanted to go to college. Regardless of Gene's protests, Tyler left his family home and chose to pursue the unknown.

Later in this chapter, the author describes how she and her brother bonded over his collection of CD's. Before Tyler left, he gave some of his favorite CD's to Tara.

PART 6: FOLLOWING TYLER'S FOOTSTEPS

Tara describes here how her older sister Audrey also decided to follow Tyler's footsteps and left home. Audrey left home when she was only fifteen. Since she had a driver's license and worked two jobs, Audrey did not need to conform to Gene' constraints and could be independent.

Later in this chapter, Tara describes how she helped her father Gene in his scrapping business. At the same time, Faye gave up her midwife business because she kept experiencing migraines and memory loss. The author describes how her brother Richard used to hide in the basement in order to read an encyclopedia.

PART 7: THE PROVISION BY THE LORD

The author opens this chapter with the description of a harrowing incident involving her brother Luke.

During one hot, rainless summer, Luke was helping his father Gene to impale cars with large skewers in order to drain them quickly of gasoline. Luke did not notice that his pants were drenched with gas. When he lit the cutting torch, they burst into flames.

Tara tended to Luke, who was suffering from third-degree burns. In order to ease the pain and to prevent the infection of the leg, Tara wrapped his leg in black plastic and then asked him to put it into an empty garbage can. After that, Tara filled the can with water and added ice.

PART 8: WORKING AS A BABYSITTER

In order to escape work in the junkyard, Tara began working as a babysitter in town. In addition, Tara took a second job, which included helping a businessman. On one occasion, Tara signed up for dance classes. Later, Faye decided to sign Tara up for singing classes. Everyone was in awe of Tara's beautiful voice. Even Gene was captivated with her voice and encouraged her to pursue singing.

PART 9: PERFORMING A LEAD SINGER

Here the author describes how she performed as the lead singer in Annie. This happened back in 1999. After that, she performed in numerous other theatre productions. Her father was certain that Y2K would collide with the Days of Abomination. Gene warned everyone that everything, including electricity and telephone lines would cease to function at the end of the year.

Sometime later, Tara met a boy named Charles. He attended some of her plays. Even though Tara was attracted to him, she decided to keep it a secret from her family.

PART 10: THE APOCALYPSE DID NOT HAPPEN

Since the Y2K apocalypse did not happen, Faye suggested a road trip to Arizona in order to lift Gene's spirits. When they got to Arizona, Gene recovered. However, while there Gene got into a fight with his mother concerning seeking help for her bone marrow cancer. Gene then insisted on returning home at night, despite the threat of an incoming storm. During the night, they had another car accident. After the accident, Tara's neck was paralyzed. Shawn, her brother who had returned some time earlier to help Gene get back on his feet, helped Tara by swiftly jerking her head.

PART 11: ANOTHER NEAR-FATAL INCIDENT

In chapter eleven, Tara wrote about yet another near-fatal accident from her childhood. Here Tara described how a domesticated horse she was riding suddenly went berserk. Her foot was stuck in the stirrup. Tara hung onto the saddle horn until Shawn came to her rescue.

PART 12: SADIE

This chapter reminisces about Tara's brother Shawn and his mistreatment of Sadie.

Sadie was a beautiful girl who fell in love with Shawn. Her brother would make her get him something and after that tell her to get him something else when she returned. He would do that continuously.

PART 13: SEPTEMBER 2001

Here the author describes the events around September 2001. Just around the time of the terrorist attacks, which occurred in September 2001, Tara hit puberty. During that time, she experimented with makeup, as she wanted to catch Charles' attention (who was unfortunately, attracted to Sadie). After Shawn broke up with Sadie, Charles has the opportunity to ask Sadie out for dinner.

Shawn did not like Charles's attention to Sadie and lashed out at Tara. During that time, Shawn physically abused Tara. However, Tyler came home in order to stop him. On the following day, Tyler told Tara that she should enroll in college.

PART 14: SHAWN HAD AN ACCIDENT

In chapter fourteen, we read about Shawn's accident. One day, during work on a construction job with Gene, Shawn survived a severe fall. Even though he recovered from the fall, Shawn developed a cruel and sadistic personality afterwards. Sometime later, Tara began studying for the ACT.

PART 15: 22 OUT OF 36

Here we read how Gene made life harder for Tara. He announced that he did not support her plans to enroll in college. Gene used parts of the Scripture in order to try to manipulate Tara and to make her feel guilty for leaving him and her previous home. At the end of the chapter, we read that Tara managed to score 22 out of 36, while the average ACT score was 20.8.

PART 16: HER SECOND ATTEMPT

At the start of the chapter, we read that Shawn hit a cow while riding a motorbike. Thus, he suffered another head injury. However, instead of taking him home, Tara asks a family friend to take Shawn to the hospital.

Tara's second attempt at the ACT is much more successful than her first attempt was. She managed to score a 28, which was enough for her to secure admission to BYU.

PART 17: COLLEGE EDUCATION

The author starts describing her college education. She enrolled in college at the age of seventeen. Tara describes how she felt alienated from her roommates, because they practiced less a rigid form of Mormonism. They wore clothes Gene would never approve of. When the author sees them at Sunday school, she decides to sit away from them.

Later we read about the courses the author signed up for. These were English, American history, music, and religion.

PART 18: READING THE BOOKS

Tara soon realized that she could not pay rent, tuition and living expenses without a scholarship. Here the author wrote how she began to panic that she would fail a grade. After one of her classmates told her that she was supposed to read the book and not just look at the pictures, her grades started to improve.

PART 19: THE FIRST JOB

Tara took a job at a grocery store during semester break. However, Gene demanded she help him with the scrapping. Since Tyler was unable to help, Tara quit her job at the grocery store and returned to Gene.

Here we also read that Shawn had developed a peaceful temperament. He was now studying for his GED, because he wanted to study law at a community college. Later Tara learned that she had scored an "A" in every subject except Western Civilization, which allowed her to obtain half of a scholarship.

During this time, Tara also pursued a romantic relationship with Charles and decided to wear a pair of women's jeans for their date.

PART 20: LEADING A DOUBLE LIFE

The author then began to lead a double life. She worked with her father and her brother during the day and after that spent time with Charles. Once, after she returned from her date with Charles, Shawn appeared and started taunting her, calling her "Nigger." Tara could not tolerate this nickname, because in college she learned about people like Emmett Till, Rosa Parks, and Martin Luther King. Tara learned about the dark history of slavery and that slavery was much worse than her family had made it out to be.

PART 21: TAKING THE PILL

Here we read that for the first time in her life, Tara took a pill for an earache. Her mother had tried to use a herbal remedy first, but it proved to be useless.

After she returned to BYU, she decided to move to an apartment off campus. This time, Tara was much more used to the "worldly" ways than she was before. She had no trouble with her music and religion courses. However, her algebra was not so good. During this time, Tara developed stomach ulcers, but refused to see a doctor.

PART 22: CANNOT PRETEND ANYMORE

Tara's relationship with Charles begins to weaken one night after he came over for dinner. Shawn had been bullying her throughout the entire evening and even physically assaulted her in front of her boyfriend. However, Tara could not pretend anymore. She could no longer lie and pretend to be someone she was not. Regardless of that, Shawn continued bullying her whenever he had the chance.

PART 23: COUNSELLING SESSIONS

Here Tara describes how during this time she regularly visited a bishop for counseling sessions. She needed it because she noticed her lack of romantic interest in any man who expressed interest in her.

When she developed a severe pain in her jaw due to a rotted tooth, the bishop encouraged her to apply for a government grant. She eventually agreed and received $4,000, which was more than enough to pay for her dental work.

PART 24: EXPERIENCING LIFE IN NEW WAYS

Since Tara had more than enough money to enjoy life a bit more than she used to, she experienced life in a new way. During one of her Psychology lessons, Tara learned about bipolar disorder and became obsessed with it. Every symptom she read about seemed to match Gene.

Tara decided she would not return home during the summer. She moved to a new apartment in another part of town where nobody knew her. During this time, Tara began a new relationship with Nick. He was a boy who fascinated Tara with his normalcy. When she developed a serious throat infection, Nick encouraged her to see a doctor. After being diagnosed with strep and mono, Tara decided to take their penicillin treatment.

PART 25: TERRIBLE WORKPLACE ACCIDENT

Tara hurried home after she found out from Audrey that Gene had suffered a terrible workplace accident. A tank full of fuel exploded when he tried to move it, which left Gene with severe burns on his lower face and fingers. Faye tried to make him go to hospital. However, Gene insisted that he would rather die than to see a doctor.

PART 26: SHAWN'S PLANS

Here we read about Shawn's plans to marry Emily. She was his long-time girlfriend. Tara broke up with Nick after she failed to be honest with him about her family.

PART 27: NEW INTERESTS

When she returned to BYU, Tara discovered new interests: history, politics, and world affairs. One of her professors encouraged her to apply to a study abroad program at the University of Cambridge. Tara accepted his advice and applied.

Six months after the accident, Gene recovered and regained his ability to talk. Gene described his recovery as God's miracle.

Sometime later, Emily gave birth to little Peter despite the fact that her pregnancy was not quite to term.

PART 28: KING'S COLLEGE

The author arrived at King's College, Cambridge. Tara was amazed by the university's grand architecture and the sophistication of its formal dinner parties. She felt insecure and underdressed next to her fellow BYU students. However, she succeeded in impressing her supervisor, Professor Jonathan Steinberg. He told her that she should pursue graduate school and that he could help her secure admission.

PART 29: RETURN TO BYU

Tara returned to BYU. Professor Steinberg sent over an application for the Gates Cambridge Scholarship and Tara was shortlisted shortly after.

Later, Faye and Gene paid her a visit at BYU. Gene embarrassed Tara by loudly talking about how the Jews had engineered World War II and the Holocaust in the restaurant.

Tara won the scholarship.

PART 30: EDUCATION AT TRINITY COLLEGE

During this time, Tara began her graduate education at Trinity College. However, she felt out of place in the company of elite British students. During December, Tara returned home to discover that Faye's business with herbal medicine had become very successful. This allowed Faye to earn a lot of money and to become rich.

PART 31: FITTING IN

In this chapter, we read how the author slowly learned to fit into life at Cambridge. She even accepted an invitation for an Italian course mate. At first, Tara was overwhelmed and even intimidated by the rich culture and history of Rome. However, she eventually began to feel at ease.

During her visit to Rome, Tara received an email from Audrey. The e-mail said that Shawn had been physically abusing Audrey as well and that she wanted to stop Emily from becoming another victim. Audrey wanted Tara and herself to report Shawn's behavior to Gene. Tara agreed but told Audrey to do nothing until she returned.

PART 32: RETURN TO BUCK'S PEAK

Tara returned to Buck's Peak. Shortly following her return, her paternal grandmother died, after which Gene lost his enthusiasm for Faye's herbal business. Later, Gene and Faye argued about "husband and wife roles."

PART 33: PLACE TO STUDY FOR PhD AT CAMBRIDGE

During this chapter, the author describes how she won a place to study for a PhD at Cambridge. She decided to write about Mormonism for her PhD dissertation. Tara bonded with her course mates and at the same time, felt distanced from her family. Regardless, Tara returned home for Christmas. After she returned home, Shawn told Tara something very disturbing about Audrey.

PART 34: VIOLENT BEHAVIOR

Tara did everything she could in order to get her dad recognize Shawn's violent behavior. However, regardless what of Tara did or said Gene refused to believe her. When she asked Faye for support, she also remained silent. Later, Gene called Shawn who threatened Tara with a bloody knife. At the end of this chapter, readers discover more about Gene and Shawn, their sadistic and cruel behavior and Faye's lies.

PART 35: EXCOMMUNICATION

After Tara returned to Cambridge Shawn started to threaten her over email and phone calls. Shawn eventually excommunicated her, saying how she betrayed him and told lies about him. A little later, Tara received a letter from Audrey. The letter stated that Audrey needed to forgive Shawn. Otherwise, the entire family would be destroyed. However, after Gene visited Audrey and brainwashed her with religious gibberish, Audrey started to believe that Tara was the one who was dangerous and provoking.

PART 36: DO YOU WANT TO RECEIVE OUR BLESSING?

Here we read how Faye and Gene visited Tara at Harvard and how they stayed in her dormitory. They wanted to give Tara their "blessing," which should "absolve her of her sins." However, Tara refused. This caused Faye and Gene to leave in anger.

PART 37: LOSING THE FOCUS

Not long after her parents left, Tara lost her focus at university. She even stopped attending classes for her French group. Tara worried that she would lose both her family and her education. Because of that, she decided to return to Idaho in order to receive the "blessing" from her dad. She then read her mother's emails, which Faye had sent to Erin. During this time, Tara realized that Faye shared the same twisted belief that Tara has been "corrupted by the devil." Tara took her journals and left. Tara decided to cut off contact with her parents for a year. She needed healing as she was suffering from panic attacks.

PART 38: UNIVERSITY COUNSELLING SERVICE

Tyler decided to defend Tara's and his own narrative. At the same time, Tara decided to enroll in the university counseling service. She found a renewed commitment to her PhD work and eventually managed to settle on her topic. The name of her PhD work was- "The Family, Mortality, and Social Science in Anglo-American Cooperative Thought, 1813-1890." Her PhD was accepted and she moved to London with Drew, who was her new boyfriend.

PART 39: VISITING MATERNAL GRANDFATHER AND TYLER

Tara returned to Idaho for some time in order to visit her maternal grandfather and Tyler.

Tara learned that Faye and Gene's herbal empire was still growing despite the fact that Gene kept continuously firing people. She met with her family and the meeting went better than Tara expected.

PART 40: EDUCATION IS OVER

This is the final chapter of the book. Here we read about how Tara did not see her parents after her grandmother's funeral. Tara remains close to Tyler, Richard, and Tony. After living with years of guilt, Tara finally accepts that she is "not the child Gene raised but he is the father who raised her." She described her new self, which was born the night Shawn physically attacked her when she was 16, as educated.

ANALYSIS

"_Educated: A Memoir_" is an autobiographical literature in which the author, Mrs. Tara Westover, describes her past life. Even though some readers might say the author was not "old enough" to write an autobiography, it is most certain that they will change their mind after they start reading the book.

The book is divided into forty chapters of different lengths. Every chapter is about one or several key events, which the author believed she needed to write. Some chapters are short, while others are longer. However, there is not a single chapter that could be considered "too long" or too boring to read. Every chapter fits "just fine" in the whole book.

When it comes to the author and her writing style, one thing is important to say here. The author makes things very simple, very clear, and very easy to understand. Because of this, the book is very easy to read and to follow, regardless of great number of chapters. When all put together it can be deduced that "_Educated: A Memoir_" has many excellent qualities. Hence, it is recommended for readers to read the full content, especially if they are interested in autobiographical books.

QUIZ

Welcome to our short quiz about the "*Educated: A Memoir*" book summary. Do you want to test your knowledge about the book? If you do, this is your favorite part of the summary!

QUESTION 1

Where did the author live after her PhD was accepted and what did was the name of her last boyfriend from the book?

a) The author moved to New York, her last boyfriend was Barry.
b) The author moved to London, her last boyfriend was Tyler.
c) The author moved to London, her last boyfriend was Jack.
d) None of the answers is correct.

QUESTION 2

When Tara develops a serious throat infection, Jimmy encourages her to see a doctor.

TRUE   FALSE

QUESTION 3

Before Tyler left his parents' home to pursue the unknown, he left something that was very precious, both to him and Tara. What was that?

    a) It was a pair of plastic figurines.
    b) Tyler left Tara his CD's.
    c) It was a Playstation 3 console.
    d) It was one music CD.

QUESTION 4

"Tara's second attempt at the _____ is much more successful than her first attempt was. Now she managed to score _____, which was enough for her to secure admission to _____."

QUESTION 5

Who was Sadie?

    a) Sadie was a close friend of Tara and Tyler's ex-girlfriend.
    b) Sadie was an ex-girlfriend of Tara's brother Shawn.
    c) One of Faye's coworkers is named Sadie. She was a girl with whom Gene had an affair.
    d) None of the above answers is correct.

QUIZ ANSWERS

QUESTION 1 – d

QUESTION 2 – FALSE

QUESTION 3 – b

QUESTION 4 – ACT, 28, BYU.

QUESTION 5 – b

CONCLUSION

"*Educated: A Memoir*" is an autobiographical book written by Tara Westover. In this book, we can read about Tara's past life, difficulties, hardships, and the challenges she had to endure and overcome. What is most important, is that Tara eventually succeeds and proves that success in life is possible, regardless of what circumstances may be. Inspirational, deep, clear and precise, "*Educated: A Memoir*" is a book that will influence and affect you in many ways.

Thank You and more...

Thank you for taking the time to read this book, I hope now you hold a greater knowledge about *Educated.*

Before you go, would you mind leaving us a review on where you purchased your book?

It will mean a lot to us, and help us continue making more summaries for you and for others.

Thank you once again!

Yours warmly,

Further Readings

If you are interested in other book summaries, feel free to check out the summaries below.

1- Summary—Hillbilly Elegy by Instant-Summary
https://www.amazon.com/dp/B076Q9VQN5/

2- Summary—Thinking, Fast & Slow by Instant-Summary
https://www.amazon.com/dp/B078GPP7T5

3- Summary—The Gift of Imperfection
https://www.amazon.com/dp/B0776RSTY9/

4- Summary—All the Light We Cannot See
by Instant-Summary
https://www.amazon.com//dp/B07653T57B/

5- Summary—The Obstacle is the Way
by Instant-Summary
https://www.amazon.com/dp/B075PFY8CP/

*For more book Summaries, visit:

https://www.amazon.com/s/ref=nb_sb_noss?url=search-alias=aps&field-keywords=instant-summary

Made in the USA
Middletown, DE
24 January 2019